IT'S TIME TO EAT AVOCADO TOAST

It's Time to Eat AVOCADO TOAST

Walter the Educator

Silent King Books
A WhichHead Entertainment Imprint

Copyright © 2025 by Walter the Educator

All rights reserved. No part of this book may be reproduced in any manner whatsoever without written per- mission except in the case of brief quotations embodied in critical articles and reviews.

First Printing, 2024

Disclaimer

This book is a literary work; the story is not about specific persons, locations, situations, and/or circumstances unless mentioned in a historical context. Any resemblance to real persons, locations, situations, and/or circumstances is coincidental. This book is for entertainment and informational purposes only. The author and publisher offer this information without warranties expressed or implied. No matter the grounds, neither the author nor the publisher will be accountable for any losses, injuries, or other damages caused by the reader's use of this book. The use of this book acknowledges an understanding and acceptance of this disclaimer.

It's Time to Eat AVOCADO TOAST is a collectible early learning book by Walter the Educator suitable for all ages belonging to Walter the Educator's Time to Eat Book Series. Collect more books at WaltertheEducator.com

USE THE EXTRA SPACE TO TAKE NOTES AND DOCUMENT YOUR MEMORIES

AVOCADO TOAST

It's time to eat, hooray, hooray!

It's Time to Eat Avocado Toast

It's green and creamy, soft and bright,

A tasty treat, oh, what a sight!

We start with toast, so warm and brown,

Crispy edges, nice all around.

Then comes something smooth and green,

The yummiest thing you've ever seen!

Avocado, soft and bright,

Mash it up, so fresh and light.

Spread it thick, from side to side,

A happy snack we won't let slide!

A pinch of salt, a squeeze of lime,

This toast will taste just so divine!

Some like pepper, some like cheese,

Or even honey, if you please!

Brother takes a little bite,

It's Time to Eat Avocado Toast

His eyes get big, "Oh, what delight!"

He nods and smiles, licks his lips,

And takes another, bigger dip!

Sister tries a crunchy slice,

She says, "Oh wow! This tastes so nice!"

She adds tomato, red and bright,

A rainbow toast, what a sight!

Mom and Dad both take a bite,

They say, "This snack is just so right!"

"It's full of goodness, smooth and fun,

A healthy snack for everyone!"

Avocados help us grow,

They give us energy to go!

Good for tummies, good for brains,

Eating them brings happy gains!

It's Time to Eat Avocado Toast

So when it's time to eat again,

Make some toast, my little friend!

Mash, spread, and top with cheer,

A snack to love all through the year!

Now our plates are nice and clean,

Avocado toast was such a dream!

Thank you, toast, so crisp and bright,

For making snack time feel just right!

It's Time to Eat

Avocado Toast

ABOUT THE CREATOR

Walter the Educator is one of the pseudonyms for Walter Anderson. Formally educated in Chemistry, Business, and Education, he is an educator, an author, a diverse entrepreneur, and he is the son of a disabled war veteran. "Walter the Educator" shares his time between educating and creating. He holds interests and owns several creative projects that entertain, enlighten, enhance, and educate, hoping to inspire and motivate you. Follow, find new works, and stay up to date with Walter the Educator™

at WaltertheEducator.com

www.ingramcontent.com/pod-product-compliance
Lightning Source LLC
LaVergne TN
LVHW052010060526
838201LV00059B/3955